Exploring
Our
Solar System

MARS

Michelle
Lomberg

AV2

www.av2books.com

Step 1
Go to **www.av2books.com**

Step 2
Enter this unique code

BVYHK2VZX

Step 3
Explore your interactive eBook!

AV2 is optimized for use on any device

Your interactive eBook comes with...

Contents
Browse a live contents page to easily navigate through resources

Audio
Listen to sections of the book read aloud

Videos
Watch informative video clips

Weblinks
Gain additional information for research

Try This!
Complete activities and hands-on experiments

Key Words
Study vocabulary, and complete a matching word activity

Quizzes
Test your knowledge

Slideshows
View images and captions

... and much, much more!

com

Exploring
Our
Solar System

MARS

CONTENTS

Introducing Mars

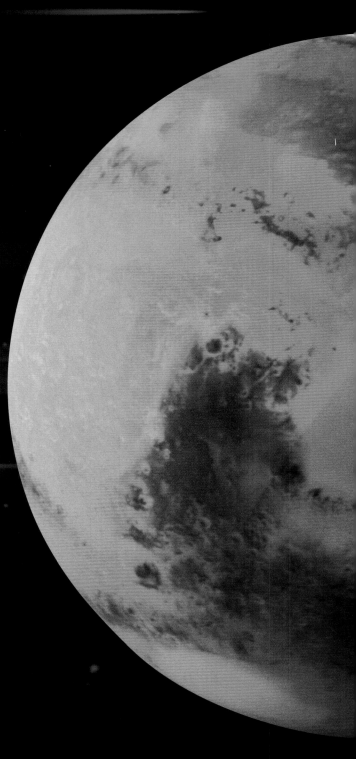

Mars is one of the eight planets in Earth's **solar system**. It is known as the Red Planet. This is because rust-colored dust causes it to appear red.

Sky watchers have observed this planet since ancient times. Mars has been the subject of **myths** and stories for thousands of years. In recent years, many movies have been made about Mars. Read on to discover more about this fascinating planet.

MARS
Red Planet Facts

Orbit

Mars makes one **orbit** around the Sun every 687 Earth days.

Dust Storms

Dust storms are common on Mars. These storms can last for months.

Rocky Planet

There are three types of planets in the solar system: rocky planets, **gas giants**, and **ice giants**. Mars is a rocky planet.

Naming the Planet

Mars was the name of the Roman god of war. Ancient Romans named the planet after this god because of its color. They thought the planet was the color of blood.

Astronomers in India also thought the planet was the color of blood. They named Mars *Mangala*. This name is linked to the Hindu war god, *Kartikeya*. Chinese astronomers noticed the bright color of Mars as well. The Chinese name for Mars means "fire."

Martian Moons

Mars has two small moons that orbit the planet. Each moon is about the size of a small town. They are two of the smallest moons in the solar system.

The Martian moons are named after two sons of the Greek god of war, Ares. The sons were named Deimos and Phobos. *Deimos* means "terror," and *Phobos* means "panic."

Phobos is the larger of the two moons. It orbits 3,700 miles (6,000 kilometers) above the surface of Mars. This is a closer orbit than any other known moon. Phobos completes three orbits around Mars each day. It takes Deimos 30 hours to complete one orbit.

Astronomer Asaph Hall discovered and named the two moons of Mars in 1877. He was working for the United States Naval Observatory at the time.

Mars

Deimos

Phobos

First Sightings

Early astronomers recorded the first sightings of Mars thousands of years ago. However, these people could not make sense of the path Mars traveled through the sky. Mars appeared to move in different directions at different times of the year.

In the late 1500s, Danish astronomer Tycho Brahe used math to track the position of Mars. Later, astronomer Johannes Kepler used Brahe's work to chart the path Mars follows in its orbit around the Sun.

Johannes Kepler outlined the laws that affect how planets move through the solar system.

Tycho Brahe calculated the position of Mars in the sky before the telescope was invented.

Cracks on Mars

American astronomer Percival Lowell was born in Boston, Massachusetts, in 1855. In the 1890s, he became interested in studying Mars.

In 1894, Lowell built the Lowell Observatory in Arizona to study Mars. He believed that the cracks on Mars were canals. He thought they proved that there had been life on Mars. Lowell's theory was proven wrong when **NASA**'s Mariner 4 spacecraft flew past Mars in 1965.

Today, astronomers continue to study space at the Lowell Observatory.

Spotting Mars

The average distance between Earth and Mars is about 140 million miles (225 million km). The distance changes as the planets orbit the Sun. Sometimes, Mars is about 35 million miles (56 million km) from Earth. When Earth and Mars are on opposite sides of the solar system, they are about 250 million miles (400 million km) apart.

Every two years, Earth passes between the Sun and Mars. This is called a Mars opposition. Mars is very bright in the sky during an opposition. At these times, the planet can be seen all night.

Earth

Mars

See For Yourself

You do not need a powerful telescope to see Mars in the night sky. Mars looks like a bright red star. Unlike a star, Mars does not stay in one place. Mars and Earth are always moving in relation to one another. This causes Mars to appear in different places when seen from Earth.

Venus and Mars can often be seen together as two bright spots in the night sky. Mars appears just below Venus.

Mars in Our Solar System

Earth's solar system is made up of eight planets, five known dwarf planets, and many other space objects, such as **asteroids** and **comets**. Mars is the fourth planet from the Sun.

VENUS

MERCURY

EARTH

SUN

Dwarf Planets

A dwarf planet is a round object that orbits the Sun. It is larger than an asteroid or comet but smaller than a planet.

Moons are not dwarf planets because they do not orbit the Sun directly. They orbit planets and dwarf planets.

Order of Planets

Here is an easy way to remember the order of the planets from the Sun. Take the first letter of each planet, from Mercury to Neptune, and make it into a sentence. **M**y **V**ery **E**nthusiastic **M**other **J**ust **S**erved **U**s **N**oodles.

ARS

SATURN

NEPTUNE

JUPITER

URANUS

Ceres

Pluto

Haumea

Makemake

Eris

Mars and Earth

Mars and Earth have many common features. Like Earth, Mars has mountains and **icecaps**. Still, Mars is much colder than Earth. The temperature on Mars can drop as low as –225° Fahrenheit (–153° Celsius) at the poles.

Gases in the air on Mars would poison humans. People could not live on Mars without spacesuits to protect them from the **atmosphere**. Astronomers believe that Mars was once more like Earth. They think the planet lost most of its atmosphere over millions of years.

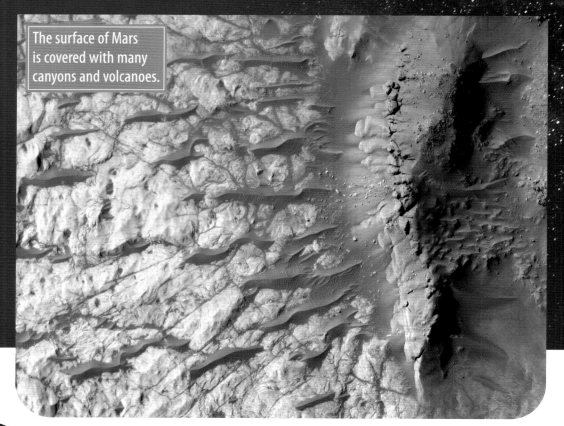

The surface of Mars is covered with many canyons and volcanoes.

Comparing the Planets

Planets (by distance from the Sun)	Distance from the Sun	Days to orbit the Sun	Diameter	Rotation Period	Mean Temperature
Mercury	36 million miles (58 million km)	88 Earth Days	3,032 miles (4,879 km)	1,408 hours	333°F (167°C)
Venus	67 million miles (108 million km)	225 Earth Days	7,521 miles (12,104 km)	5,833 hours	867°F (464°C)
Earth	93 million miles (150 million km)	365 Earth Days	7,926 miles (12,756 km)	24 hours	59°F (15°C)
Mars	142 million miles (228 million km)	687 Earth Days	4,221 miles (6,792 km)	24.6 hours	−85°F (−65°C)
Jupiter	484 million miles (779 million km)	4,331 Earth Days	88,846 miles (142,984 km)	10 hours	−166°F (−110°C)
Saturn	891 million miles (1,434 million km)	10,747 Earth Days	74,897 miles (120,536 km)	11 hours	−220°F (−140°C)
Uranus	1,785 million miles (2,873 million km)	30,589 Earth Days	31,763 miles (51,118 km)	17 hours	−320°F (−195°C)
Neptune	2,793 million miles (4,495 million km)	59,800 Earth Days	30,775 miles (49,528 km)	16 hours	−330°F (−200°C)

Mars Today

Astronomers have sent many **space probes** to perform flybys, orbit, and land on Mars. The most recent mission to Mars is InSight, which landed on the surface of Mars in November 2018. It is studying the geology of the planet. Another Mars mission is the Mars Science Laboratory, called Curiosity. Curiosity is a **rover** that landed on Mars in August 2012. It is currently exploring the planet's surface looking for signs of past water or life on Mars.

Mars Odyssey
Launched 2001
Vehicle Orbiter

Mars Express
Launched 2003
Vehicle Orbiter

MAVEN
Launched 2013
Vehicle Orbiter

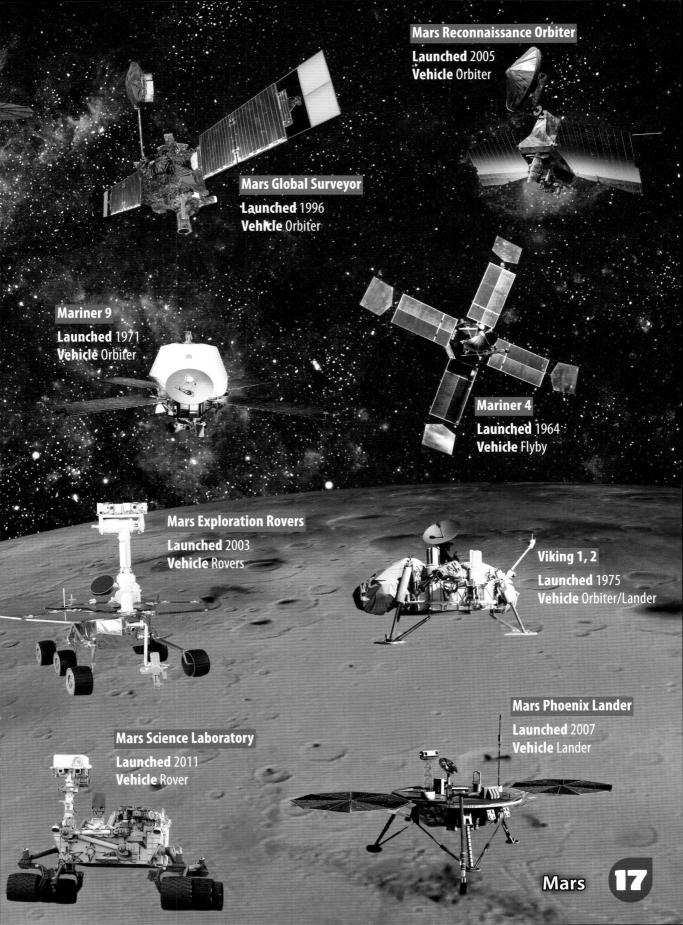

Mars Reconnaissance Orbiter

Launched 2005
Vehicle Orbiter

Mars Global Surveyor

Launched 1996
Vehicle Orbiter

Mariner 9

Launched 1971
Vehicle Orbiter

Mariner 4

Launched 1964
Vehicle Flyby

Mars Exploration Rovers

Launched 2003
Vehicle Rovers

Viking 1, 2

Launched 1975
Vehicle Orbiter/Lander

Mars Phoenix Lander

Launched 2007
Vehicle Lander

Mars Science Laboratory

Launched 2011
Vehicle Rover

Giovanni Schiaparelli discovered cracks on Mars

Giovanni Schiaparelli (1835–1910) was an Italian astronomer. He saw long cracks on the surface of Mars. Schiaparelli called these lines *canali*. This word means "channels" in Italian. People thought that Schiaparelli had discovered water canals like those built by humans. A strange idea began to spread. Some people thought that space aliens had built the canals.

Some scientists now believe that the lines Giovanni Schiaparelli called *canali* are ancient riverbeds.

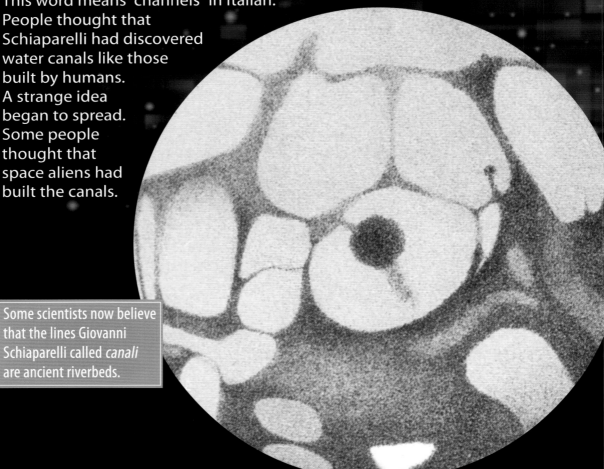

Bob Mase guides Mars space probe

Bob Mase works at NASA. He was the first lead **navigator** of the space probe Mars Odyssey. Mase worked with a team of NASA scientists. Together, the team guided the space probe in its orbit around Mars.

Mase grew up in Florida. His childhood home was close to NASA's Kennedy Space Center. This gave him an interest in space from a young age.

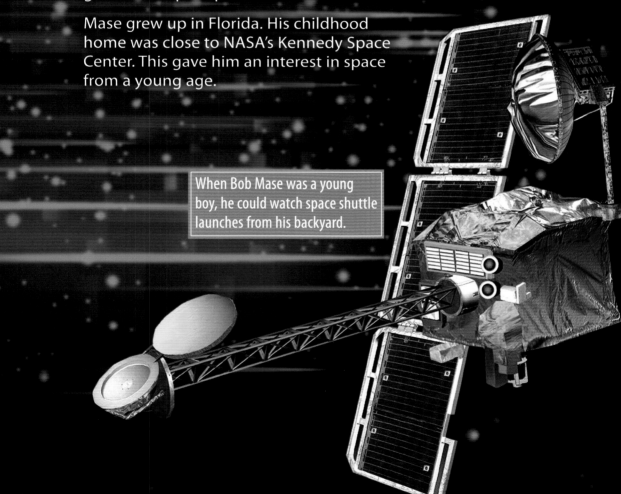

When Bob Mase was a young boy, he could watch space shuttle launches from his backyard.

YOUNG SCIENTISTS AT WORK

Calculate Your Weight on Mars

Your weight depends on gravity. Gravity is the force that pulls objects toward a planet's center. Mars has less gravity than Earth. This means that you would weigh less on Mars than you do on Earth.

To calculate your weight on Mars, find your weight on Earth and multiply it by 0.4.

NASA's Curiosity rover weighs 2,000 pounds (907 kilograms) on Earth. On Mars, it only weighs 800 pounds (363 kg).

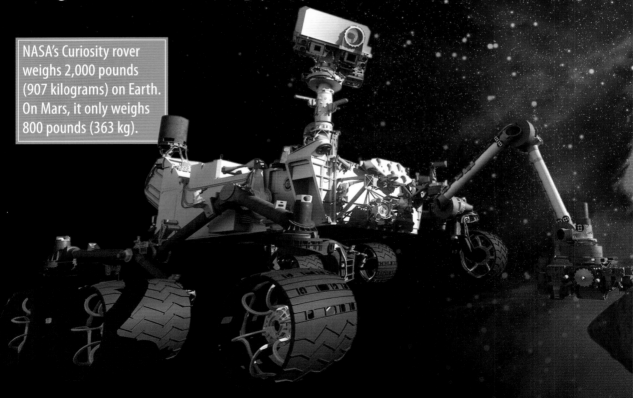

MARS
Red Planet Facts

Water on Mars

Scientists think that Mars had water on its surface billions of years ago.

North and South Poles

The north and south poles of Mars are covered in **dry ice**, which is the frozen form of carbon dioxide.

Olympus Mons

Olympus Mons is a volcano on Mars. It is the highest volcano in the solar system. Olympus Mons is 16 miles (25 km) in height and covers an area about the size of Arizona.

What Have You Learned?

1 Why is Mars called the Red Planet?

2 Where does the name Mars come from?

3 Name the moons of Mars.

4 Can you see Mars without a telescope?

5 Mars was discovered in the 1500s. True or False?

6 Is it possible for people to live on Mars without spacesuits?

7 Did Martians build canals on Mars?

8 What did Giovanni Schiaparelli call the lines on the surface of Mars?

9 Mars is closer to the Sun than Earth. True or False?

10 Earth is larger than Mars. True or False?

Answers
1. Because of its rust-colored surface 2. From the Roman god of war 3. Deimos and Phobos 4. Yes 5. False 6. No 7. No 8. Canali 9. False 10. True

Key Words

asteroids: small, solid objects in space that circle the Sun

astronomers: people who study space and its objects

atmosphere: the layer of gases surrounding a planet

comets: small objects in space made from dust and ice

dry ice: the frozen form of a gas called carbon dioxide

gas giants: large planets made mostly of gas; Jupiter and Saturn are gas giants

icecaps: large areas covered by ice, usually in polar regions

ice giants: very cold giant planets; Neptune and Uranus are the two ice giants in the solar system

myths: stories or legends, often about gods or heroes

NASA: National Aeronautics and Space Administration; the part of the U.S. government responsible for space research

navigator: a person who directs the travel of a spacecraft

orbit: the nearly circular path a space object makes around another object in space

rover: a robotic vehicle used to explore the surface of a planet

solar system: the Sun, the planets, and other objects that move around the Sun

space probes: spacecraft used to gather information about space

Index

Get the best of both worlds.

AV2 bridges the gap between print and digital.

The expandable resources toolbar enables quick access to content including **videos**, **audio**, **activities**, **weblinks**, **slideshows**, **quizzes**, and **key words**.

Animated videos make static images come alive.

Resource icons on each page help readers to further **explore key concepts**.

Published by AV2
350 5th Avenue, 59th Floor
New York, NY 10118
Website: www.av2books.com

Library of Congress Control Number: 2019951374

ISBN 978-1-7911-1736-8 (hardcover)
ISBN 978-1-7911-1737-5 (softcover)
ISBN 978-1-7911-1738-2 (multi-user eBook)

Printed in Guangzhou, China
1 2 3 4 5 6 7 8 9 0 24 23 22 21 20

022020
101119

Project Coordinator: Priyanka Das
Art Director: Terry Paulhus

Photo Credits
Every reasonable effort has been made to trace ownership and to obtain permission to reprint copyright material. The publishers would be pleased to have any errors or omissions brought to their attention so that they may be corrected in subsequent printings.

AV2 acknowledges Alamy, Dreamstime, Getty, NASA, and Shutterstock as its primary image suppliers for this title.